HOME/BODY
GEORGIA RESSMEYER

PEBBLEBROOK PRESS

an imprint of *Stoneboat*—www.stoneboatwi.com

PEBBLEBROOK PRESS

Published by Pebblebrook Press
an imprint of *Stoneboat*
PO Box 1254
Sheboygan, WI 53082-1254
Editors: Rob Pockat, Signe Jorgenson, Lisa Vihos, Jim Giese
www.stoneboatwi.com/pebblebrook-press.html

Home/Body ©2017 Georgia Ressmeyer
Library of Congress Catalog Card Number: 2017946898
ISBN: 978-0692912874

All rights reserved. No part of this publication may be reproduced or transmitted in any form or by any means, electronic or mechanical, including photocopy, recording, or any information storage and retrieval system, without the prior written permission of the publisher.

Front cover photo by Georgia Ressmeyer ©2017
Author photo ©Lisa Lehmann/LehmannPhotoArt.com

Printed in the United States

Acknowledgements

The author thanks the editors of the following journals in which these poems first appeared, some in slightly different form:

An Ariel Anthology: Transformational Poetry and Art 2014 (Ariel Woods Books, 2014): "Winter Solstice"

An Ariel Anthology: Transformational Poetry and Art 2015 (Ariel Woods Books, 2015): "The Ride"

An Ariel Anthology: Transformational Poetry and Art 2016 (Ariel Woods Books, 2016): "The Vast Impersonal," "Falling Apart," and "The Winner"

Avocet: A Journal of Nature Poems: "Gold at Day's End," "Attuned to Light"

Blue Heron Review: "A Clear Day"

The Cresset: "Absence," "Compensatory Joy"

The Four Seasons (*Kind of a Hurricane Press*, 2015): "Winter Into Spring," "Summer Doldrums"

Illuminations: An International Magazine of Contemporary Writing: "Do Not Disturb"

Museletter: "Broken," "They Hear Me Coming"

Puerto del Sol: "Cracked"

Red Cedar Review: "It May Seem Odd But It's Not"

Seems: "Sea Levels Rising"

The Solitary Plover: "Dead Leaves Invade the Patio"

Stoneboat Literary Journal: "A Poet of Dilapidated Rooms" and "To An Extrovert"

Verse Wisconsin: "Prosperity's Prison"

Wisconsin People & Ideas: "Her Statement"

Wisconsin Fellowship of Poets' Calendar 2014: "A Soul's Novembers"

Wisconsin Fellowship of Poets' Calendar 2017: "The Habit of Snow"

Wisconsin Fellowship of Poets' Calendar 2018: "Two Cranes"

In memory of
Renate Ruth Gabriella Klein
brave, outspoken niece
who refused to let her disability stifle her spirit

and

Faith Carol Ressmeyer
passionate, justice-seeking cousin
who excelled at translating beliefs into actions

1/ONE

A False Train : 12
The Vast Impersonal : 13
Winter Into Spring : 14
A Moon Half Full : 15
Lowly : 16
Time Caving In : 18
At the Motel Restaurant : 19
Cracked : 20
A Poet of Dilapidated Rooms : 21
Alone with Cancer : 22
Mother Most Present When We Were Sick : 23
On Being Driven : 24
Evolution in Reverse : 25
Habitats of Trust : 26
Giving Way : 27
Free Will : 28
Redolence : 29

College Collage : 32
Breaking Up : 33
Two Cranes : 34
Sea Levels Rising : 35
Cool Day, Rough Sea : 36
To an Extrovert : 37
Squall : 38
Human Nature : 39
Words Trail Away : 40
Summer Doldrums : 41
Her Statement : 42
Listless : 44
This morning : 45
Rummage : 46
Absence : 47
Corporeal : 48
To the Cemetery : 49
The Sparrow and the Sparrow Hawk : 50
Home Body : 51
Do Not Disturb : 52

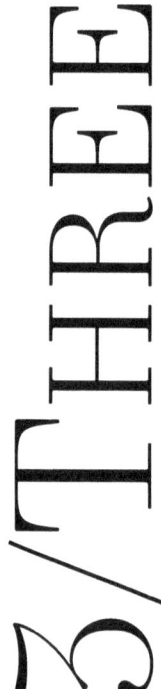

Monarch Butterflies : 54
Prosperity's Prison : 55
Addicted : 56
Weather Conditions : 57
Who Owns You : 58
When a Rose Is No Rose : 59
It May Seem Odd But It's Not : 60
Compensatory Joy : 62
Lullaby : 63
A Soul's Novembers : 64
When You Were Flush : 65
Dead Leaves Invade the Patio : 66
Extravagance of Light : 67
Thanksgiving Idyll : 68
Broken : 69
Falling Apart : 70
Gold at Day's End : 71

Breakfast in the Country, Early : 74
Jammed Thumb : 75
Winter Solstice : 76
The Habit of Snow : 77
An American History : 78
Bird Tracks in Snow : 80
They Hear Me Coming : 81
Attuned to Light : 82
The Nature of Hope : 83
Each Other's Keepers : 84
The Winner : 86
A Clear Day : 87
The Ride : 88

1/One

A False Train

A false, never-ending train clatters along
the tracks of evergreens' high branches
from one stand of trees to the next,
speeding up, slowing down,
never stopping for riders.

All who would get on or off must shinny up
or down a trunk, seize and release
an armful of needles. No one has seen
a passenger come back.

Onward the train hurtles, rustles, hisses
on trestles of branches, rushing
to wind-knows-where at unparalleled speeds,
unnerving all who live near the tracks.

Some hold pillows over their heads to soften
the din, shield them from pine cone projectiles,

as desperation quickens among those lacking
defenses against elements conspiring to
shove them off a bluff, a platform, their rockers.

Eventually a few, sapped of all desire to stay
rooted in peace-forsaken Earth, will climb trees
and hurl themselves onto that infernal,
eternally-false train going nobody-knows-where
in such a terrible, unstoppable rush.

The Vast Impersonal

The drama of blue-black clouds
over Lake Michigan, breaching
like great blue whales,
stops me from taking a step.

The sky could open its mouth,
consume me for lunch.
I'm a small fish on a small hook,
faking my decay and death—

yet thrilled to witness clouds'
prodigious, impersonal might.
I could be swallowed up—
not be apart from this, but part.

Winter Into Spring

All winter, clouds bore down on us
like stacks of mattresses we had to
carry everywhere on our heads,
our bent backs, and shoulders.

Now in spring we can't find a trace
of these burdens and wonder where
we laid them, who took them, whether
there's any residue to sweep up.

Our spines slowly readjust, causing us
to walk lighter, taller, without
scraping our feet on road salt, concrete,
and ice.

Is this some kind of trick? Will we be
pounded into the ground by falling futons
the moment we express relief?

Is blue sky just an illusion of youth,
lightheartedness, an absence of cares
that will open like a secret door
on a storehouse of ripened horrors?

We have seen and borne too much
to trust this lightness to last, that our
burdens won't be heaped back on us
at the close of the act.

And yet, while we can, we gaze upward,
admire the beauty and brightness that
had seemed so distant—for the present
not letting forebodings unhinge us.

A Moon Half Full

In the night, weird light
and a far-off thump drew me
to the sunroom, where a half-moon
flashed her mirror at the round
glass table.

Seated in a wicker chair I watched
her throw wrought-iron shadows
on the floor.

Her gaze was surprisingly bright
for one half here, half not.

The shadows she laid were unlike
any I'd seen, not straight and stark
but prone to curl, as if attempting
to complete her arc.

Needing sleep, I excused myself,
went back to bed. The moon
didn't wake me again but did fill
my dreams with visions of S-curved
necks of swans, of heavy-headed
peonies bending to the ground.

How troubled she is—and I am—
in our disdain for being less than full,
our strong desire to burn roundly,
as the sun does, with our own
unquenchable fire.

Lowly

You stoop but do not crouch
over the first patch of trout lilies
blooming in the woods by the river.

The trout lilies stoop as well,
their delicate star flowers dangling
on thread-like stems to face the ground
as if Earth and their own spotted leaves
were the most interesting objects
for study in this whole airy world.

You want to show them the wonders
of the sun and treetops and birds
in flight, but all they're able to see
are your shoes, though they do feel
the sun's warmth on their backward-
curving petals and sepals.

You decide they bend downward
because they're cold, just as in early
spring you fold in on yourself
to hold your own heat while you look
for wildflowers starting to open.

And just when you swivel your head
to gaze around, the wind may swivel
theirs, by this means allowing these
lilies to take in more than you realize.

Who knows? Maybe trout lilies are
entomologists of tiny, creeping insects,
or expert appraisers of patterned leaves
as tapestries or magic carpets.

From your perspective, their lives may
appear lowly, humble—but is yours
really any different when viewed
through the eyes of an eagle or airplane?

Time Caving In

Time caves in on me.
The rubble of recent accretions
blocks the exit, confining me
with early memories, the scrawls
on the walls of my skull.

I'm not sorry to see successes
fall—security, a tidy house,
nice furniture—but people I
want to talk with have to shout.
My own voice is giving out.

Yet here you sit beside me
on the couch in younger forms,
in more tumultuous times
whose follies and splendors I
can now evaluate sensibly.

I will address myself to memories
I can whisper with, save fuller
voice for those I bellow at
through my accumulations,
the wasted months and years I

spent not knowing who I was or
loved or what my soul knew best.
I'll shed unnecessary masks and
holler love songs to the loyal few
who listen, and who holler back.

At the Motel Restaurant

we sit next to a wallpaper mural
of a Mediterranean terrace
overlooking a harbor with sailboats—
the best fake view in the place.

My breakfast companion, half
Italian, has the gestures to match,
waving her bread with one hand,
then the other, as she talks.

Her forgetfulness is getting worse.
Conversation jumps the tracks
more often than it used to.

I remind myself that her tangents
are as important as the point I
wanted to make, the story
I hoped to complete

repeating myself as often as she
repeats, though I'm always
convinced my repetition will aid
her comprehension, which
it doesn't.

My mind is one-track, hers is
off-the-beaten. These days
they meet less often.

I tell myself to loosen up, go as
loopy as she does, always
keeping in mind that I'm not
the conductor, and life is a circle.

Cracked

We're damaged goods:
corners dented,
sides compressed,
lids scratched.

Whoever sent us
didn't bother with
Styrofoam or
bubble wrap.

The skin
we came in
proved too thin
to withstand

the blacks and blues
of being dropped,
wedged, or
crushed—

yet we function,
more or less:
we creak, try
to think, even have

inklings of affection.
We may be
marred but are
not lost

unless/until
we lose the will
not to give up—
or out.

A Poet of Dilapidated Rooms

A poet of dilapidated rooms, used
clothing stores, used books, rummages
through other people's goods until
she is discarded by discarded things

still bearing thumbprints of those
who owned them first—hats with
the presence of mind to shout her off,
signatures that by their gravity or

giddiness bar access to the contents
of books, photographs of glowering
matriarchs and patriarchs in oval frames
disdaining her and modern ways

she represents—even as she works
to integrate present with past,
honor not waste, recollect her own
displacement, dig through layers

to bedrock, never claiming ownership,
only memory, relationship, no matter
how tenuous or slight. She demands
little. She will get what she wants.

Alone with Cancer

Name-calling is risky.
Cancer might swell with rage,
proliferate vindictively.

Appeasement seems equally
chancy. Cancer must not
get off easy.

It's probably best, for now,
to exist quietly, calmly, as if
I'm in no hurry, have all
the time in the world to settle
our boundary dispute.

I shall remain silent, not rail
against my fate, my cancer,
but serenely plot to be healthy,
eat better, learn to relax.

Let the surgeon and his robot
sharpen their knives, do battle
with cancer on my behalf.

Blissfully anesthetized I'll rest
on a bluff above the fray
oblivious to success or failure.

Mother Most Present When We Were Sick

Ailing now, I need
your cool hand
stroking my forehead
as you did
when I was young.

I never appreciated you
more than I did then—
except now, though
you're seven years dead.

Dry toast, saltines,
ginger ale, tomato soup—
these I can't eat without
a thought of you,
the relief I felt when
starting to recover.

Yes, I can take care
of myself now, Mother—
but you would do it better.

On Being Driven

Taking a backseat, being driven
can feel like a blessing.

Let your eyes imbibe the landscape:
greening fields, woodlots,
hills with the soft, rounded backs
of giant animals you'd like to pet.

Sky dims, sights soften, pink horizon
sinks into darkening trees.
Farmhouse lights ignite.

White moon, nearly round, looks on
unblinking. You wish you knew
what it was thinking, though you
don't ask.

You hurtle along on engine power,
not talking, just watching life
as it pulses with and against you,
each particle at its own speed
to its own destination.

You're content to be where you are
in this instant, and the next one,
and the one after that, till you're home
in a house that kindly waited up.

Evolution in Reverse

For the sake of a recovering abdomen,
arm muscles atrophy, forbidden
to lift anything heavy, push or pull.

Shoulders sag to simian posture,
spirits slumping with them.

Back down the evolutionary track I plod,
ape on the street, caged in a house.

With effort I straighten my spine and
seek brightness: veiled sunshine above,
foliage transforming daily,
mauve azaleas,
columbines upping periscopes,
catkins dangling like fake worms from trees,
unfolding leaves.

I assume my body will perk up soon,
have its May in June.
Till then I await my evolution to human.

Habitats of Trust

A calm assault,
a tender jolt
to hibernating senses
comes courtesy of
birds billowing in
from gentler places,
returning words I
misaddressed in fall,
crumpled now but
still disowning hope.

As words come
home to roost, birds
stake out a higher
truth, make ribbons
of my lines, weave
stanzas into nests.
Transfiguring despair,
they twist my dread
to kinder use
in habitats of trust.

Giving Way

An unusual bird,
not one I've heard before,
calls from a distant
wire or branch, its

melancholy six-note trill
a descant to
downspout drips,
kitchen tocks.

My skein of thought
is drawn to it
—the song, the bird—
though not to follow,
yet.

I wonder if one day
in mist I will
meander off to chase
a ghostly string of notes
heard twice.

The thread of home could
snap inside my brain.

I could give way
to wandering.

Free Will

A cottonwood tree lies prostrate by the river,
awash in the foam of its own white fluff.

A child could bottle enough wishes here to make
one wish a day for the rest of her life.

Patches for the ozone layer! Polar bears on fields
of ice! An end to war! Chocolate for the world!

But who would wish so many wishes on a child?
The burden of choices is too great.

Even God didn't want that much involvement,
ceding the field to Satan—and to us: free will.

Selling our souls for a wish is more than most
of us can manage, and it happens only once.

Of course, the underlying intent is always
complete freedom from choice.

And it's granted. Comfort at last. Peace at last.
No complexities, moral ambiguities, need to think.

I skim the foam of options, weight them with
rocks, drown them in the river.

How fine to be as free as God again! I wouldn't
wish wishes on my own worst friend.

Redolence

Red roses in a clear glass vase
on a round glass table
of wrought iron and wicker,
two chairs, three picture windows,
African blossoms clumped
like the head of a puce hydrangea
scanning the morning paper.

Outside, purple columbines
raise their stems, their white and
purple bells to heights
previously unseen, ring in their
conquest of the yard, secretly
plot more tiny seeds to increase
their holdings.

Trees and bushes spread sideways,
grow taller, lilacs push out flowers,
birds dart all over, bees drone,
all nature hums to sun and water.

I, too, owning this moment, these
riches, imagine no other season
or blossom, am enamored of spring
with outrageous passion, revel
shamelessly in new green, in reds,
pinks, violets, and in the heady
fragrances of my lilac childhood.

2/Two

College Collage

Back at the U that wasn't you,
on acres of open, grassy space,
that rolling Indiana landscape,
someone has pasted new buildings
made of brick and glass.

So far they haven't loaded up
the sky with trees or towers
but continue to let hot sun be sun
and moon, moon.

You were impressed and not
impressed. Buildings are shelters
where learning can happen,
but dreams need vistas—
the broader the better.

It was never your U, though it was
your open space and sky,
which you hardly understood
until the clutter.

Now you carry the memory
of openness with you—
the backdrop on which each place
you've lived in, or passed through,
is pasted.

The glue will fail in the end,
the pieces fall. Only field and sky
will remain.

Breaking Up

A robin, no respecter of sleep
or variations on a tune, repeats his same
perky phrases endlessly outside
my window, sounding as if he's perched
on my pillow in the predawn mire
of dreams, where I'd rather linger.

I don't need further exposure
to the nuances—few—of his song.
It sounds pleasant enough at dusk
and when he returns in spring
but only annoys at 4 a.m.

Why target me for these early serenades?
I don't have feathers, build nests, lay eggs
—and, if I did, I certainly wouldn't sit
on them or feed worms to nestlings.

I admire his energy and hygiene, his
frequent dips in my birdbath, but this
boisterous predawn crooning has to stop.

I'm fond of you, Robin—just not that way.
Please do yourself a favor and find
an early-rising, egg-laying partner who's
as wild about worms and your singing
as you are.

Two Cranes

Slicing sky's blue silk
   with sharp bills
     straight necks
cranes open seams

Day's fabric curls
  like wake
    diverging streams

I'm towed behind
    cranes' silent
       mated flight

until—my eyes
    too weak—I
drop the rope of sight

Sea Levels Rising

When Lake Michigan climbs the bluff
claws her way up up up past riprap
dropped to stabilize the bank she
clutches weeds saplings the trunks of
trees she hauls her dripping body to
the top stops to admire the view from
an Adirondack chair in someone's yard
moves into a mansion for a brief respite
swims in the indoor pool with zebra
mussels still clinging to her green
algae-tangled hair sleeps in a queen-
size bed surrounded by windows that
crack from the roar of her outsized snore
tries to make a fire but can't find
a dry match finally gives up bursts
through the front door rushes across
the lawn to the street where she flows
gradually west seeps into every home
liberates tropical fish gushes up a slope
until she comes to a single-story flat-
roofed house almost square in shape
which she lifts from its foundation
and tows like a toy in her wake while
an old woman sits inside at a small desk
pen in hand sifting her brain for
something remarkable to recount to her
sister in a nursing home five states away
not even noticing a change in the view
though she does feel a bit more adrift
than usual and can't help wishing
something extraordinary would happen
to make her letter more exciting but
so far nothing has and she doubts it will

Cool Day, Rough Sea

A pod of white pelicans
puddles on a limestone shelf
which shrinks as waves, birds
compete for standing space.

Pod swells, swells swell.
Stone's commandeered by froth,
white necks, white breasts
bright orange feet, yellow bills.

More pelicans squeeze in—
blind spots in white,
angelic messengers of south,
tidings of desired warmth.

To an Extrovert

Who you blew kisses to mattered—
to them as well as me.

You blew kisses promiscuously,
spread them across the land
like far-flung spores—

whether to say hello, goodbye,
convey thanks or love, I never knew.

Kisses flew off your fingertips like
jets—nothing delicate or fluttery
in your technique

but passionate, indiscriminate,
come one, come all.

Your gestures, never small, flung bits
of you to everything and everyone
in sight.

I would have liked to save you
for myself—

but when you stopped pitching kisses,
nothing I trusted was left.

Squall

A bald eagle worries seagulls
on their nests;
they worry him back,
chase him to the tip of a pine
which pricks him as he sits.

He spreads his outsized wings
to drive them off,
then soars away.

The racket of the squealing gulls
grows faint.

The squall, no longer ominous,
glides swiftly to the lake.

Human Nature

In what tangle of vines and shrubs
unpruned by any hand but wind's
will I find the design
for this mood?

It's lopsided, unruly, cannot be
teased by eyes into even the most
rudimentary order or beauty,

remains convoluted, ingrown,
an affront to the sight of every gardener,
artist, or parent who's been bitten
by a desire to improve on nature,

must be uprooted to be tamed
but will clasp in its claws
enough earth to regenerate itself
wherever it's dropped.

This mood is fierce, defiant, unyielding,
will haunt its limbs and roots if any
succumb to a lopper or backhoe.

Better adjust to the snarls of its structure.

Best to let nature be nature.

Words Trail Away

She talks to herself
off and on

leaves gaps where
silence enters

gusts in one ear
out the other

Words trail away
as if
her horse is faster

when really she
slogs along
like a tortoise

plodding to mold
sand into sense

Summer Doldrums

All day I wait
for a flicker of weather
a blink
toe-tap
strand of hair slipping
out of a barrette
facial tic
hint of breath

Death is
wax
cement
shellac

In time I'm sure to get
a second wind
come dancing from
my grave
mood
to match a lively gust
if gusts resume

Do gusts forget?

Will I remember
every step?

Her Statement

Yesterday morning I'm pretty sure it was yesterday
I started walking along the beach toward someone who
would meet me at my destination. Where it was or
who it was I can't remember off the top of my head.

I'd walked that way a hundred times before and knew
my feet would take the right path through the woods
when the rocks became too high to climb.

Near some bushes that leaned into the path I sat down
to tie my shoe. Then I saw wild raspberries growing
over my head and ate a few. They tasted so much like
lunch that I figured this must be my destination
and stayed for a long time eating and waiting.

Then night came and I heard boys shouting laughing
and cursing as they climbed the rocks. I could tell
they were not for me so I curled up and slept
on the overgrown path.

There were rustlings in the woods all around me and
once a soft tail or whisker brushed my cheek but
no one came to meet me.

In the morning I crawled back out to the beach and sat there on a pile of rocks to watch the sun come up. I could see its heart beating in the shimmer of its giant orange eye. My own eyes beat in time with it and somewhat cried.

Later a woman came and said she would walk me to the street which she did and then I went up and down each one until I found a house that fit the key on the ledge at the top of the door. I came inside and I was here. And that is everything I know about what happened.

Listless

Oh, there are lists—
damp ones, not snappy,
beyond anyone's capacity
to complete and
cross off with a flourish.

Even birds seem
sapped of purpose,
their chirps indifferent,
songs fading
without resolution.

Air hangs in a blur,
gauzy, unmoving.
Where is day going?
Nobody cares.
Not a soul will follow.

This morning

crisper light, edges of leaves
cut out by sharper scissors
waving on stems to blue sky
squeezed dry of excess moisture
by a popular front that slunk
through town on solstice night,
wrung her diaphanous black
scarf, hung it up to dry,
then left a spectacular mark—
a strawberry moon that swung
in a great arc on gravity's string,
while in my bed I rolled from
side to side, dreamt of berries
exploding sweetly on my tongue,
woke to the cool inhalations
of an open window, pulled a thin
blanket over my skin, sunk back
into the soft mattress of foam
from which, this cool a.m.,
I sprung refreshed, I sprung!

Rummage

You try something on at a rummage sale
something not particularly stylish

and it fits and is comfortable and you
think you're becoming that way too

so you buy it for warmth or gardening
or to wear on your whimsical days

assuming you can find that state again
and it hangs on a hanger or sits on a shelf

for months and you start to wonder "What
was I thinking when I bought that scrap?"

until one day you put it on just for fun
and abruptly the magic takes hold and you

rush out of the house looking strange yet
totally yourself and you think "What a fool

I was!"—which you were and will stay,
though at least today it's completely okay.

Absence

Your absence, like the prodigal's,
cannot be touched.

Distractions cover loss with
moss and frill, but loss
is bottomless.

Hope does not light my sorrow
from below.

On metal chairs in entryways
I wait for you:

your swinging arms,
your singing voice,
your breath against my cheek.

I wake. I wait for you. I sleep.

Corporeal

The desolation we feel when a loved one
    is taken too young, too soon,
the rending of our hearts like temple veils,
the distress we experience when goodness
cannot or will not save itself or be saved
    from evil or accident or illness,
the grief of the Marys for their dead Jesus—
losses like these we reel from while we're
still corporeal: hands we cannot squeeze,
    cheeks not kiss, bodies not enfold.

Spirit lives on, yes, but not the small miracles
of daily meeting: talking, walking, eating,
    touching, laughing, looking.

We must go on without our loved one's
fleshly presence. How can we? We ask this—
    and for a long time hear no answer.

To the Cemetery

To find your way to the cemetery
of lost loved ones

take a path by the sea or a pond,
a patch of wild roses, an evergreen wood,
a cornfield, a row of wind-beaten houses

take with you a fistful of photos
of bygone poses, smiles, hairstyles

take a right or a left or go straight
from the cemetery gate to the plot
that loosens or thickens

take away withered flowers or grasses
blighting your view

take a new photo of the headstone
for your headstone collection

take time to reflect on the life or lives
at your feet, how they shaped and
chipped away at your inborn traits

take a moment to pray, or address them
directly, say what you wish you'd said
to a listening presence

take a different path home, wipe dust
from your shoes,

take a deep breath to renew
your existence as you.

The Sparrow and the Sparrow Hawk

I have seen God in the sparrow
and the sparrow hawk
squeezing it to death.

I have watched the sparrow's lights dim
and go out as talons pierced its chest—
God slaying God in my backyard,
a sacrifice of flesh
sustaining life.

This is not war's slaughter,
putting on God's armor for power
or salvation's sake, storming Heaven's gate
to seize control by force.

This is sparrow and sparrow hawk,
the daily communion of predator and prey:

this is my body, this is my blood,
given for you, shed for you; remember me.

Home Body

This is my body

memory in tow
on a frayed piece
of rope

only routine
keeps me in line

wandering mind
loosening grip

God save the ship
all hands on deck

habit to pilot us

Do Not Disturb

When calm returns—
and by calm I don't mean
dull sheen, limp wind,
the suspension of breath

I mean air moving
rhythmically in and out
of my chest,
a respite though brief

from sweltering thought,
the illusion
even if quick to disperse
of freedom and strength—

when calm like that returns,
don't wake me.
Please.

3/Three

Monarch Butterflies

You're crumpled in the surf,
half buried by sand.
Do you have a death wish?
An unquenchable thirst?

Your black legs cling to my
fingers when I scoop you out
and brush the stubborn
granules from your wings.

I carry you into the dunes
and try to set you down
on goldenrod, out of
the clutches of your confidant

and nemesis, the wind,
but you will not release my
life-raft hand. When you do
let go, you spread your wings

above the sand. Whether
they're sound enough to pose
for field-guide photographs
or hopelessly torn, my message

to you is the same: rest now
and save your strength. You'll
need it for your next wild ride,
that next impossible drink.

Prosperity's Prison

In prosperity's prison, managing
gadgets is the business of life.

What a price my soul pays—
so burdened with stuff that it gasps
and wheezes in the lonely dark
of packing boxes, plastic bags,
padded envelopes—

longing to slip through the cracks
to a patch of sunlight
in an empty space.

Oh, for a life of nothingness—
my soul says, and I say—

rich in drift-potential on currents
of air or water, going nowhere
slowly,

infinitudes of beauty all around me,
the life of a vagrant, panhandling
freedom from vagabond clouds

allowing nothing smaller than Earth
or Galaxy to hold my gaze
or play the mystic music of my
nights and days.

Addicted

To be transported to a better place
to an altered state we drink alcohol
eat cake meditate smoke tobacco
marijuana have sex binge on chocolate
sip espresso fall in love drive too fast
gormandize pop a pill guzzle soda
inject heroin read books play games
watch movies text incessantly
exercise too much sleep too little
write poems listen to music sing songs
dance till dawn get high on our own
natural chemical imbalances—so who's
to say what is or isn't an acceptable trip
when we're all addicted to something
or someone, and most get away with it?

Weather Conditions

The moment I realize I'm dressed
too warmly for the weather, am about
to take my windbreaker off and tie it
around my waist by its slippery sleeves,
a rush of wind blows a ghost-train of fog
down the cross-street before me,
impelling the ancient silver maples overhead
to unleash a cascade of drops that douse
my neck in streams.

Shivering and hugging myself, I wonder
if I'll be too cold at the beach, though I'm
relieved not to suffer from heat as I did
a minute ago.

Suddenly the chilly, fog-propelling,
drop-expelling gust stops dead in its tracks,
the train vanishes, and the moisture
on my neck begins to evaporate.

I'm disappointed, thinking I've missed my train,
though the fog in my brain settles
comfortably into its own padded seat.

I resume my journey to the beach on a caboose
of my own musing, neither too cold nor too hot,
oblivious to all but the churn of my feet.

Who Owns You

The pocked and furrowed brow
of the sky, its thousands
of eyes, don't threaten directly
but disconcert.

You wouldn't call them ominous,
though they study you with
detached exactness, which
might turn into disapproval.

Just in case, you tell yourself
not to make any sudden moves,
break into a run, swing your
arms unduly.

You're being watched by more
eyes than you realize. Is it
best to play it safe? Your god
has been erased—

and not just by Santa Claus.
Belief and being good aren't
enough to get you the world
you want, deliver you from evil.

Make waves wisely, never
letting the ones who think they
own you rule your thoughts.
You own you. Nobody else.

When a Rose Is No Rose

A long cane of a rosebush—
the one that wants only to climb,
clawing its way up without
support, putting all its effort
into height—

scrapes my windowpane
with thorns like fingernails
on chalkboard, scratching
my brain, trying to draw color
as crimson as the rose it lacks,
make me the rose of it—

but what a rose: ill-tempered,
ready to lop us off at the knees
to find relief from the chafe
of abrasive thoughts like these.

It May Seem Odd But It's Not

Try telling that to your regular clientele who
come into your tiny shop looking for something
quaint in quotes or creative in quotes—
a pair of gloves covered with buttons, say, or
an orangutan mask made of toilet paper tubes—
and instead all you stock this week are books
with green covers or predominantly green
cover art, causing your customers to ask in
petulant tones what is the meaning of this
to which you respond I have gone completely
green, I am making an environmental statement,
and of course then they lecture you on how
many trees it takes to print a book and you say
these books are all recycled and they say I can't
give my sister a used book for her birthday
and you say yes you can if it's outrageously
expensive, and their eyes light up and they
want to know how expensive and you say
that depends whether you want me to track down
Edith Wharton or Willa Cather and have her sign
or inscribe the book to your sister, or I can affix
an approval sticker from the Sierra Club or
maybe Robert Redford—and naturally you get
the sale eventually but you begin to question
whether this is the most efficient way to clean out
your library so you busy yourself again making
buttonhole placemats and scratch-paper purses

and other items from junk you find lying around
the house or in the street, all of which can be
assembled and sold with minimal effort or expense
on your part and so your little shop soon gets
back to normal in quotes having nothing
the least bit odd about it, and no ma'am, you
tell them, I've gone back to selling just my original
artwork in quotes and other one-of-a-kind
conversation starters yes gift-wrapped gratis by
the artist of course!

Compensatory Joy

If you estimate autumn's peak
leaf by leaf as lily-lover God
must—hairs-on-your-head,
sparrows-in-freefall God—
you don't discount what is
for what's expected,
single note for crescendo,
firecracker for grand finale
but stand under the branches
of each tree and watch
the flush of greeting spread
lobe by lobe, leaflet by leaflet
until you know by a slow
process of accretion one
lingering, compensatory joy
in the otherwise impossible job
of being, and staying, God.

Lullaby

Tuck your feathered
bodies into the folds
of rocks to doze.

Choose clefts beyond
the reach of waves
and slithering creatures.

Nestle into worn
hollows in Earth's
limestone lap.

Nap with an ear to
the air for the flap
of predators' wings.

Do not sing out or
chirp in your sleep.
Dream of a warm,

deserted beach with
millions of small
crustaceans to eat.

Rest, brave migrants.
The sky will quiver
when it's time to wake.

A Soul's Novembers

What sun in dismal rain
sets my garden's soul flaring?
It glows with its own gold fire,
self-contained, requiring no
external combustion.

Sparks fly out from a maple's
crown, spiraling down like birds,
stoking precious flames
in a bed of coals as cold rain
pelts the earth.

There's no extinguishing my
garden's sun, even when a rake
scatters or snow covers
its embers. Wind always finds
and fans a soul's Novembers.

When You Were Flush

When you were flush
your hands dripped honey.

Everything you touched
stuck to your fingers.

Thick, sweet, amber were
days you remember.

Now you taste ash, grit,
mouthfuls of silt.

Whatever you clutch
slips from your grip.

Yet you *sense* and decide
life is a taste—any taste—

on your tongue. You're
alive with just one.

Dead Leaves Invade the Patio

each leaf rigor-mortised
a clenched fist
more crunch than punch

small brown birds
hunched on patio squares
exhausted, lost

crumpled lunch bags
crows once munched from
wind-tossed

bunches of rats
plotting assaults
on the house

all skitter and scatter
helter-skelter
edged with frost

Extravagance of Light

Ambiguous November grays
give way to gold-plated water,
heaven's broad-brimmed indigo hat,
wave foam being blown back
by sand-filled whops of wind
or streaking sideways
like a ripped-out hem.

Fists and ropes of mussels
in their weedy grass-green nets
dab the rain- and wind-swept
beach where frozen sand crunches
underfoot and puddles twist
the sun's rays and wind strokes
into rippling fish-scale filigree.

Pink-legged herring gulls
devour a large dead fish whose
fins and tail appear to have been
dipped in blood

as dogs and walkers wag their tails
in crisp delight—for all is good
and clean, rinsed and scoured
by the storm, then draped
in an extravagance of light.

Thanksgiving Idyll

On Thanksgiving Day, if I show up at the cottage
the family sold before my parents died,
will they still greet me at the door
with hugs and loving words?

Will Dad preach a grateful sermon at St. Peter's
Lutheran Church, Mom play the organ while
the turkey roasts?

Will they be well, not needing walkers, shaking,
anxious, or confused? Will Daddy not repeat
himself?

Will my three siblings suddenly appear,
and will we laugh and get along before our
parents' memory loss, Parkinson's, and cancer
drag them down? us down?

Will I be social, not retreat into another room?
Will Mommy interact, command our help,
laugh at all of Daddy's jokes?

Will there be candles and a fire, good music, best
china, silverware, a lovely meal? Will all of us
be better than we were, less driven, happier?

Will love and thankfulness prevail?

This time we cannot fail.

Broken

Red roses dangle from a soul's lattice
heavy-headed, necks broken.

The soul accepts proliferation,
sharp thorns, sacrifice.

Accepts—or expects?
No one knows.

Attend to the broken: rose windows, all.
There are temples everywhere.

Falling Apart

Bound to matter
by fragile ties:

a coffee cup, its anemic
contents, clutched to
my chest till the house
heats up

slippers re-stitched with
remnants of shoestrings
kept in a jar

a gel pen leaving inkless
impressions of script
on scraps of paper

and peace in my airspace
peace in my heart

the things of this life
like old friends

falling apart

Gold at Day's End

Windows and trees
gilded like facades
and artifacts of
palaces, churches

inestimable riches
in twigs, leaves that
never asked to be
so grand or blessed

who have the best
of gold without
a need for guards or
preservation, whose

grasp on wealth is
open-palmed, as
from these spill coins
that melt to crown

the tallest trees last,
which gladly glow
then throw their riches
west to where the sun's

low rays still glint
of gold—true wealth
just passed along, not
seized or hoarded.

4/Four

Breakfast in the Country, Early

Slowing down for sun-glittered frost
on the overpass

as you take a blast in the eyes from
the up-glowing orb

on a country road with no other cars
only golden grass

is to be blessed by a small child with
maple syrup

on her cheeks who is filling your face
with one round eye—

a bedazzlement you carry with you
in your own happy smile

on your own sticky face for the rest
of the drive

warmed by coffee, French toast, the
unexpected sparkle of your joyous host.

Jammed Thumb

A jammed right thumb has lost its grip
on reality
begins to oppose its own opposability
refuses to assist
in twisting lids off jars
or pouring orange juice from a carton

Its anti-contrarian rebellion
its puffed-up pride in being less utilitarian
would seem comical if not for
the slight ache it creates when pressed
into service on a task as light
as cradling a pen

Then what a squall of a scrawl that thumb
makes
taking advantage of a loosened grip
to loop wider write taller
than more sedate fingers appreciate

although at the end of the page
its point successfully made
the anti-opposable thumb settles down

inspiring hand and mind to decide
wisely it seems
to break where the breaking is clean

Winter Solstice

Cedars seize the sun for ransom,
clutching her fierce, bulbous body
in scaly evergreen hands.

Beams slink free to flash sun-messages
on clouds: that she will rise
to heat this hemisphere again.

Deep snow, sun's low trajectory,
ephemeral days, long-huddled nights
lend only cave-hard sleep, yet

one hope gleams from hostage rays
and spires of distant stars: life flares,
desiring—always—to be ours.

The Habit of Snow

Sky in the habit of snow
does not cloister well.
We wish she'd be as pure
as the driven, but she isn't.

She goes roaming at night,
shrieks wind-chants off-key,
scatters her potion
of ice shards and crystals—

only to emerge the next day,
a glow in her cheeks,
to lift us from snowbanks
with the kindness of a saint.

An American History

She was never a client, never the subject
of an active case, just a woman who was housed,
thirty years ago, on the top floor
of the mental health center in long-term care
with no hope or expectation of ever getting out—
an angel, I thought, who'd been dropped there
by mistake.

The first time she called my office it was to ask
if I could please make the hospital stop forcing her
to have so many babies. She'd already given birth
22,000 times, which, she said, was exhausting.

Later she called to say that the hospital had removed
part of her brain—"the happiness memories
of my childhood"—and could I please
find a surgeon who would put them back.

She told me she'd recently seen a little girl
in the canteen whom she knew to be her own.
"We have the same eyebrows," she said. Then she
added, "Normally when I'm with children my voice
goes into the high registers, but today I was like
a little, dead leaf."

Once she invited me into her room to show me
her "Christmas Card to the World," signed
with her full name and displayed on her dresser
year-round. She told me she'd given money to
all the countries of the world to take care of the poor.
"The rich can take care of themselves," she said.

She let me look at her books, which included
War and Peace and a novel by Henry James—
though she hadn't been able to finish these—
a Bible, a book about the Bible, and a history book.
"I really like to read books about the American
History," she said.

Another time she called and told me, "Some
people think I'm the Virgin Mary. I don't know
if it's true, but Joseph of Bethlehem says I look
like her. I'm trying to marry Joseph of Bethlehem,
except I don't know whether he's going to
come through for me or not."

Although I never did find a surgeon who could put
the "happiness memories" of childhood back
in her brain, she was always gracious to me,
and grateful for any attention I paid her—as I was
to encounter her generous spirit.

Years later, in response to an important court decision,
the hospital's long-term care units were emptied out,
their residents moved to community placements.
Today I like to picture my non-client living contentedly
among her books and other precious possessions
in a group home or supervised apartment.

But who knows: Maybe Joseph finally came through
with a proposal. Maybe the two are happily married
and living in Bethlehem, with babies she's allowed
to keep.

Bird Tracks in Snow

In the simple script of bird tracks in snow,
a story is told.

I was here, it says, looking for seed.
I hopped on the top, peering and pecking.
The snow was too deep.
I found nothing.

For people who feed birds, this story brings
guilt for not getting out sooner
to shovel and fill feeders,
or despair when snow falls so fast
we can't keep up.

We read the story over and over.
The tiny tracks of juncos and finches,
the larger ones of doves,
are imprinted in our minds like lines
from favorite books.

We're hungry, they say. We have nothing
to eat.

So out we go to fill the void—
for a moment, at least.

They Hear Me Coming

How could they not? I'm wearing snowshoes.
The crunch these make on frozen snow
is as loud as walking on seashells.

Seven deer stare as I round a bend in the woods.
All stop in place, almost close enough to touch.
All are curious. They've seen me before,
know my reassurances.

I treasure the moments when deer and I
comfortably cohabit the animal kingdom,
share creaturely traits—inquisitiveness,
for example—without fear.

We address each other with our eyes, all
seeming to say, "Life is good. I'll take a chance
and trust you with mine, at least today."

Attuned to Light

Light fights for us
and does not lose
even when no one's
in the woods to observe,
splits air like a hatchet
loud as the crack
of a branch to the owl
who's sitting on it,
jabs chickadees to sing
who'd gone silent
in the woods—
saving their breath,
keeping cold out—
needling them now
to practice spring's
repertoire on anyone
or no one pausing
under a pine to listen
to familiar sounds
from birds who never
left and never lost
the simple tones light
tuned them with
inestimable breaths ago.

The Nature of Hope

This is the downslide of winter,
the softening that lasts.

Hope packed in chests
is cautiously unwrapped,
held to the light,
inspected for cracks.

All repairs will be made in March
when hope is placed on a shelf
in a glass-fronted case
for safekeeping.

Hope is a fragile object
hand painted in bright,
blossomy colors,
cherished, rarely forgotten.

Occasionally one of us drops it.

The handle stays missing.

Each Other's Keepers

He was tormented when I met him years ago:
snakes everywhere, electrocutions, explosions,
dark circles under his eyes, pants falling down,
hadn't eaten in days, attempted to suffocate his mother
with one hand—or so the police report claimed—
though he said he'd been trying to protect her
from breathing poisonous fumes.

When we sat down to discuss the commitment case
against him he asked, "What would *you* do if you went
down into the basement of your house and you saw
there were three people trapped in the furnace
with a boa constrictor and none of them had eaten
in a week?"

He said there were bombs going off all around him,
exploding under his feet. He could hear the explosions
a second apart. I asked if the sounds he heard
might possibly be the beat of his own heart.

"No," he said, without anger, pointing at the floor,
"it's coming from down there." At one point he told me
to take my hand off the table because it was being
electrocuted and turning brown.

He said he had three big worries about staying
in the hospital: his dog, who required medical attention;
his mother, who was old and weak and needed him
around the house; and the people in the furnace, who
had to be gotten out.

At his request we telephoned his mother. She was
elated to hear he was taking medication again.
She asked if he would have to stay in the hospital long.
"I'm an old woman," she said, "and frail. It's hard
for me to get along without him."

When I handed the phone to my client, he spoke
to his mother calmly at first, then gradually became
hostile, ranting about Communists and accusing her
of stabbing him in the back. But as he returned
the phone to me he whispered, "I didn't mean
a word I just said."

Later that day his mother called and told me he was
fine when he took meds. "He cooks for himself,"
she said, "takes out the garbage, puts my storm
windows up. I do his laundry but he pays me for that."

Then she added, "All we have is each other.
There's no one else to talk to."

Mother and son were reunited a week or so later—
minus toxic fumes, explosions, captives trapped
in the furnace—thanks to effective pharmaceuticals
and the cooperation of many.

The Winner

Who will be the winner of this day?
Will it be unrelenting gray and damp?
an aching knee?

Grief—will it be that?
A late arrival on the internet
of sad news from overseas?

Might it be a slant of hope—
a robin pulling up a worm?
the first spring flower opening?

Will my headache rise above my head,
lift my spirits on a silver thread?

To win, hope need not cross a finish line
but offer only slight relief to me.

Then what a crown I'll make for it
of thatch, pine cones, and dried reeds.
I am not difficult to please.

A Clear Day

Arched, white-cloud eyebrows,
the sun's one Cyclops eye
give the sky a look of astonishment
at seeing Earth so clearly
after days of veiled views.

All cataracts have been removed.
We of Earth, scattered across
the landscape, stare upward
with similarly startled expressions,
unused to seeing so much blue.

Mutual admiration fills the air—
fireworks of joy emanating
from the sun and from our faces
at this sudden expansion
of prospects.

Beauty has found us. Squirrels
celebrate with feats of gymnastics
on rooftops and fences. Birds chirp
from bushes. Hearts leap to see
smiles on the faces of those we love.

How can we make this last? Can
we shellac every shining juniper,
each laugh? No, but we can absorb
them through our eyes, ears, skin.
We can remember them. We can!

The Ride

The wind puffs up;
it flaps and untraps you.

You fly before it
on an even keel.

Your veins thrum
with exhilaration, wonder.

Who knew you had it in you
to glide so fast and far?

Wind does the propelling;
you hold the tiller, steer
for dear life.

In due course the air will
drop you back to Earth,
or below it.

Till then you glide with
grace you've been granted,
glad for the ride as you go.

Wind and water are my favorite elements, probably because I spent my childhood summers swimming and sailing on Long Island's North Fork. Now I live three blocks from Lake Michigan in Sheboygan, Wisconsin. This is not a coincidence.

Field guides are among my most treasured possessions. Literary biography, fiction, and poetry also feed my spirit. At home I am surrounded by books, which I enjoy holding in my hands to read.

Time spent alone has always been essential to my happiness and inspiration, whether I'm roaming beaches, dunes, prairies, or forests or sitting in a sunny, private spot reading or writing.

I majored in history at Valparaiso University in Indiana, then lived for a year in Tokyo, Japan, where I taught English at a women's junior college and several companies. After that I attended law school at Yale.

Following graduation I settled in Milwaukee, Wisconsin, and went to work as a legal services attorney. I also served as an organizer and legal consultant for a coalition of feminist groups. For eighteen years, I was a staff and managing attorney with the Milwaukee Mental Health Division of the public defender's office—a dream job in many ways, although occasionally that dream was a nightmare.

Since 2002, I have lived in Sheboygan. Here, and throughout Wisconsin, I have found a lively and supportive community of poets, artists, and other friends. Here, too, I revel in the drama and solace of a Lake that is truly Great. This place feels like home.

I write poetry because I have to. Through poetry I make sense, or nonsense, of my experiences and honor the natural world I find so welcoming. As I age, my life is more often complicated by health challenges and the deaths of people I love. These events make it deeper and richer. I have no regrets.

Georgia Ressmeyer

www.ingramcontent.com/pod-product-compliance
Lightning Source LLC
Chambersburg PA
CBHW071200090426
42736CB00012B/2403